On Location NYC

New York City's Top 100 Film and TV Locations

ALEX CHILD

© 2013 Museyon Guides

Published in the United States by:
Museyon, Inc.
20 E. 46th St., Ste. 1400
New York, NY 10017

Museyon is a registered trademark.
Visit us online at www.museyon.com

ISBN 978-0-9846334-6-3

1359219

Printed in China

I love films.
I love photography.
I love New York!

Walking down the streets I enjoy finding filming sites and taking photos.
Although I sometimes experienced a hard time finding places such as the street from *Léon: The Professional* or the rooftop from *Across the Universe*, chasing old billboards and researching background scenes usually solved the problem.

I decided to include many New York landmarks and streets with New York flavor, and movies that were highly acclaimed or won Oscars and other awards. I believe that this book is good for tourists as a walking tour guide or a New York souvenir. For New Yorkers, it offers a way to see the city through movies.

And…Action!

Alex Child

KEY: TOP 100: **0**, RESTAURANTS & BARS: Ⓞ,
SEX AND THE CITY: **0**, SMASH: **0**

SCENES FROM NEW YORK CITY

"Boy, this is really a great city, I don't care what anybody says—it's really a knock-out, you know?"

MANHATTAN (1979)

58th Street & East River
Sutton Place

When Isaac (Woody Allen), a 42-year-old TV writer, meets Mary (Diane Keaton), a mistress of his best friend, he is initially turned off by her snobbery. But then he runs into her again at a party at the Museum of Modern Art and shares a cab ride home with her. They walk her dog and chat until sunrise at the East River, where they realize they get along better than they originally thought. The iconic scene of the couple's silhouettes under the Queensboro Bridge, with George Gershwin's "Some One to Watch Over Me" in the background, is one of the most beloved moments in New York City film history. It wasn't an easy shot to get, however. The scene was filmed at 5 a.m., and required the crew to bring their own bench.

Map: Page 114 **9**

"I am not going to say it again. I am not going to say it again."

KRAMER VS. KRAMER (1979)

The Mall, Central Park

Since the Kramer family lives on the Upper East Side, Central Park is Billy's (Justin Henry) playground. The park's tree-lined Mall appears two times in the movie. In the summer, Billy tries to ride a bicycle for the first time with help from Ted (Dustin Hoffman). Later Billy sees her mother Joanna (Meryl Streep) in winter, fifteen months after she left the family. The movie swept the Academy Awards in 1979 and became an important milestone in the careers of both Dustin Hoffman and Meryl Streep.

Map: Page 126 44

When Harry Met Sally... (1989)

Katz's Delicatessen
205 East Houston Street

One of the most unforgettable scenes in movie history is Sally's (Meg Ryan) dramatic performance at Katz's Delicatessen. Over pastrami sandwiches, Sally tries to convince her longtime friend Harry (Billy Crystal) that men can't tell when women "fake it." Her logic? "It's just that all men are sure it never happened to them and all women at one time or other have done it so you do the math." Then she expressively proves her point as other customers watch. When she finishes, a woman nearby places her order: "I'll have what she's having." Today a sign marks the spot.

"Are you the last person in New York still taking out library books?"

SEX AND THE CITY: THE MOVIE (2008)

New York Public Library

When newspaper columnist Carrie Bradshaw (Sarah Jessica Parker) visits the New York Public Library to return the book *Love Letters of Great Men*, she decides it would be the perfect venue for her wedding to her longtime off-and-on paramour, Mr. Big (Chris Noth). But on the big day, an overwhelmed Big has second thoughts. Devastated, Carrie flees the wedding and attacks Big with her bouquet on 40th Street between Fifth and Sixth avenues, adjacent to Bryant Park. In reality, Carrie would have never returned a book here; the Schwarzman Building is a research facility. A lending library branch is across the street.

Map: Page 118 ③

"Okay. Should we get some coffee?"
"Sure…Where?"

FRIENDS (1994–2004)

The Friends Apartment
90 Bedford Street at Grove Street

Rachel (Jennifer Aniston) moves into Monica's (Courteney Cox) apartment after running away from her wedding to her fiancé, the dentist Barry. Their sprawling two-bedroom apartment became the main stage of one of the most popular American sitcoms of all time. Who can forget the series finale when everyone leaves a copy of their keys on the counter on the way out to Central Perk for yet another cup of coffee and a new chapter in their lives?

Map: Page 136 **67**

"You can do whatever you want with your life, but one day you'll know what love truly is. It's the sour and the sweet. And I know sour, which allows me to appreciate the sweet."

Vanilla Sky (2001)

Times Square

Vanilla Sky starts with an aerial shot over Manhattan that moves over buildings, Central Park, and finishes at the Dakota apartment building where the rich bachelor David (Tom Cruise) lives. David wakes up, grabs a list, watch, and a driver's license, and drives a Porsche to Times Square, only to find it completely empty—not a single person is in the so-called "crossroads of the world," where approximately 300,000 people pass daily. Capturing this impossible scene was no CGI trick, however. It was filmed at the crack of dawn one Sunday morning in November, while the square was shut down for just three hours with help from New York mayor's office and police department.

Map: Page 118 **25**

"Do you mean sleep over?"
"Well, yeah."
"OK…but I get to be on top."

BIG (1988)

FAO Schwarz
767 Fifth Avenue at 58th Street

The famous scene where Josh (Tom Hanks), a 12-year-old boy trapped in the body of a 30-year-old man, and toy magnate Mr. MacMillan (Robert Loggia) play "Heart and Soul" and "Chopsticks" on a giant piano was filmed at the FAO Schwarz toy store. On the day of filming, stuntmen were on hand just in case the two could not do the dance moves correctly, but the actors were determined to do the entire keyboard number without the aid of the stuntmen. They succeeded. Shoppers can still dance on the legendary Walking Piano on the second floor of FAO Schwarz—or take it home with you for $250,000.

Map: Page 114 **⑬**

"So what? So plenty! I love you, you belong to me!"
"No. People don't belong to people."

BREAKFAST AT TIFFANY'S (1961)

Tiffany & Co.
727 Fifth Avenue

Early one morning, a yellow cab pulls over at Tiffany's on Fifth Avenue. "Moon River" plays in the background, as the car approaches from the south (in reality Fifth Avenue runs in the opposite direction). Dressed in pearls and a black Givenchy gown, Holly Golightly (Audrey Hepburn) steps out onto the street and nibbles a pastry and sips coffee while window-shopping at the iconic jeweler. Today it is one of film's most famous scenes, but it could have turned out very differently. Instead of the gamine Hepburn, the part was first offered to the bombshell Marilyn Monroe.

Map: Page 114 14

"Every morning I still wake up and the first thing I want to do is to see your face."

P.S. I Love You (2007)

Holly and Gerry's apartment
254 Broome Street

As the movie opens, Holly (Hilary Swank) and Gerry (Gerard Butler) appear from the East Broadway subway station and argue over an incident at dinner as they walk back to their apartment on the Lower East Side. Gerry dies suddenly of a brain tumor, but not before arranging messages ending with "P.S. I love you" to be delivered to Holly after his death. The letters send her on a journey to Ireland, as she slowly regains the confidence to love again.

Map: Page 142 **75**

"When you read a book as a child, it becomes a part of your identity in a way that no other reading in your whole life does."

YOU'VE GOT MAIL (1998)

Zabar's
2245 Broadway at 80th Street

On Thanksgiving Day, Kathleen (Meg Ryan) goes shopping and mistakenly ducks into the cash-only line at Zabar's, a gourmet food store, to hide from her business competitor, Joe (Tom Hanks). Surprisingly, Joe helps Kathleen deal with a difficult cashier and heckling customers, without the two realizing that they have been flirting via e-mail. Like many of the locations in the film, Zabar's is an Upper West Side institution, and the film paints a charming picture of the neighborhood. Other true-to-life locations include the characters' apartments, and the romantic Café Lalo.

Map: Page 130 55

"My friends and I are making a very large withdrawal from this bank. Anybody gets in our way, gets a bullet in the brain."

INSIDE MAN (2006)

20 Exchange Place

Dalton (Clive Owen) and his gang have come up with a foolproof plan to rob a bank. Their target? Manhattan Trust Bank near Wall Street. They lock the doors and take hostages and then finally request two buses and an airplane to escape. Detective Keith Frazier (Denzel Washington) is assigned to negotiate with Dalton, but the case is more complicated than it seems. The Hanover Street entrance of the building at 20 Exchange Place was used as a main entrance for the bank. "It looked like the perfect bank robbery. But you can't judge a crime by its cover."

Map: Page 152 **91**

"I will be at the South Street Seaport everyday at mid-day, when the sun is highest in the sky."

I AM LEGEND (2007)

South Street Seaport

In 2012, virologist Robert Neville (Will Smith) is the last healthy human living in New York after a devastating outbreak. After losing his dog, Sam, in an attack by infected dogs, he takes revenge on infected vampiric humans, called Darkseekers, the following night at the South Street Seaport, running them over with his SUV. When he is nearly killed, a pair of immune humans from Maryland, Anna (Alice Braga) and Ethan (Charlie Tahan) save his life, and encourage him to continue with them to a survivor's colony in Vermont. The dramatic flashback scene to the evacuation of New York was filmed over six consecutive nights in January on the Brooklyn Bridge with 1,000 extras and various military vehicles and aircraft at the cost of $5 million—believed to be the most expensive shoot in New York film history.

Map: Page 152 **85**

-HOT SOUP-

MED   16 OZ $2.99
LARGE   32 OZ $3.99

MULLIGATAWNY
CRAB BISQUE
TURKEY CHILI
JAMBALAYA
BLACK BEAN
CHICKEN BROCCOLI
CLAM BISQUE
SPLIT PEA
FRENCH ONION
MUSHROOM BARLEY
TOMATO RICE

ALL SELECTIONS MADE
FRESH DAILY

NO SUBSTITUTIONS OR
PHONE ORDERS

-- NO --
SOLICITORS

SEINFELD (1989–1998)

Soup Nazi (The Original Soup Man)
259-A West 55th Street

One of the most famous characters from Seinfeld history, the Soup Nazi first appeared in Season 7. Although the TV version of the soup shop is a studio set, the character is inspired by the real-life owner of a shop called The Original Soup Man. On the show, Jerry (Jerry Seinfeld), George (Jason Alexander), and Elaine (Julia Louis-Dreyfus) go to a new soup stand where the owner is known as the Soup Nazi for his short temper and strong attitude to customers. By annoying him, Elaine is refused her soup and banned from coming to his stand for one year. Elaine gets revenge by discovering his secret soup recipes. "Next!"

Map: Page 118 **28**

Night at the Museum (2006)

**American Museum of Natural History
Central Park West and 79th Street**

Based on the 1993 children's book *The Night at the Museum* by Milan Trenc, the movie tells the story of a divorced father, Larry (Ben Stiller), who takes a job as a night watchman at the American Museum of Natural History to impress his son. Larry discovers the exhibits come to life at night, making him responsible for a rambunctious tyrannosaurus skeleton nicknamed Rexy, as well as the cowboy Jedediah (Owen Wilson) and his nemesis, the Roman general Octavius (Steve Coogan). While internal scenes of the museum were filmed at a sound stage in Vancouver, children and the young at heart will find plenty of magic among the museum's diorama displays.

"Civil war dudes! You guys are brothers, for God's sake. You gotta stop fighting. North wins. Slavery is bad. Sorry. Don't want to burst your bubble, but South, you guys get Allman Brothers…and…Nascar. So just chill!"

Map: Page 130 **54**

"Because of me, you have nothing."
"Because of you, I have you."

It Could Happen to You (1994)

Bethesda Terrace, Central Park

Inspired by the true story of a New York police officer who split a $6 million lottery win with a waitress, this film tells the story of police officer Charlie (Nicolas Cage), who, when left without enough cash to tip his waitress at a diner, promises to split his lottery ticket as a tip. When the ticket wins big, the lives of Charlie and the bankrupted waitress Yvonne (Bridget Fonda) are drastically changed. The pair rollerblades at Bethesda Terrace in Central Park when Charlie plunges into a pond, and they begin falling in love as their lives fall apart around them. "I told you I'd share my ticket. I never planned on sharing my heart."

Map: Page 126 **45**

ANNIE HALL (1977)

Annie Hall's Apartment
68th Street between Madison and Park Avenues

In one of the most iconic romantic comedies of all time, Alvy (Woody Allen) and Annie (Diane Keaton) first meet at a tennis court on a downtown pier. After the game she offers him a ride up to the Upper East Side, where they both live. Annie finds a parking spot on 68th Street near her apartment and the two have a brief exchange on the street, before she invites him up for a glass of wine. In the scene, the limestone buildings in the background capture the atmosphere of New York's Upper East Side, typical of Allen's films. While Annie Hall is one of film's most famous characters, her name, at least, isn't a work of fiction. Diane Keaton's real name is Diane Hall and her nickname is Annie.

Map: Page 126 **35**

TAXI DRIVER (1976)

Eighth Avenue and 47th Street

Suffering from insomnia, Travis (Robert De Niro), an ex-Marine and Vietnam War veteran, takes a job as a night-shift taxi driver. In the opening sequence, Travis goes to an adult movie theater on Eighth Avenue in the morning after work. The scene where he walks down the street with the Hollywood Theatre in the background became the famous theatrical release poster of the movie. Though the corner has changed a lot since then, it still recalls the atmosphere (and smell) of Times Square in the '70s and '80s.

"SWF seeks female to share apartment in west 70s. Non-smoker professional preferred."

SINGLE WHITE FEMALE (1992)

The Ansonia
2109 Broadway at 73rd Street

After breaking up with her boyfriend, Allie (Bridget Fonda) advertises for a roommate. She eventually settles on Hedra (Jennifer Jason Leigh), but soon finds her new roommate's horrifying true nature, as Hedra begins taking on aspects of Allie's personality. The apartment building where the thriller unfolds is itself another star of the film, its façade and stairwells played by the Ansonia on Upper West Side. It was built as a luxury residential hotel in 1899 in the lavish Beaux-Arts style. Many celebrated residents have called the Ansonia home, including Babe Ruth, Igor Stravinsky, and Angelina Jolie.

Map: Page 130 52

GHOST (1990)

Sam and Molly's Loft
102 Prince Street

Wall Street banker Sam (Patrick Swayze) and his artist girlfriend Molly (Demi Moore) move into a cast-iron building on Prince Street in SoHo. Unable to sleep the night after they move, Molly begins casting pots at 2 a.m. Sam wakes up and grabs Molly from behind, clay sliding between their fingers as the pottery wheel spins, and the Righteous Brothers' 1965 song **"Unchained Melody"** rises in the background. Their happiness is short-lived, however, as Sam is soon after murdered, and must haunt his love to uncover the truth behind his death.

"Did you know that 35 people try to jump off the Brooklyn Bridge each year, most because of broken hearts?"

DEFINITELY, MAYBE (2008)

The Pond, Central Park

When his college sweetheart Emily (Elizabeth Banks) visits him in New York, Will (Ryan Reynolds) proposes while walking in Central Park. She responds by confessing that she slept with his roommate, saying that she is "letting him go" because she is not able to share his career ambitions. In the film, the incident is one of the romantic adventures Will recalls for his young daughter Maya (Abigail Breslin), who asks to talk about his life before marriage. Though Will is in the midst of a divorce, he finds that a second look at the past may give him a second chance at the future.

Map: Page 126 **41**

"I like New York in June, how about you?
I like a Gershwin tune, how about you?"

THE FISHER KING (1991)

Grand Central Terminal

Jack (Jeff Bridges) and Parry (Robin Williams) come to the Grand Central Terminal to look at Lydia (Amanda Plummer), with whom Parry is smitten. At five minutes before 5 p.m. she appears in the crowded station and Parry follows her. Suddenly the commuters start waltzing in the main hall. This magical scene was filmed between 3 a.m. and 5 a.m. with 400 extras after hours of waltz lessons due to an urgent change of the script. The director, Terry Gilliam later said,

"I think the Grand Central Station waltz sequence in *The Fisher King* is as good as anything I've done."

Map: Page 114 **1**

"When you've been betrayed by a friend, you hit back. Do it."

ONCE UPON A TIME IN AMERICA (1984)

Washington Street and Water Street
Brooklyn

Noodles, Max, Patsy, Cockeye, and Little Dominic are a gang of Jewish kids living on the Lower East Side in the 1920s. They make their first big score, by hiding a shipment of bootlegged alcohol. After keeping the money in a locker at the train station they are attacked by their former boss Bugsy, and Dominic is shot to death on the street near the Manhattan Bridge—their happy moment suddenly turning to tragedy. The original cut by director Sergio Leone was 3 hours and 49 minutes long; the film was cut to 2 hours and 19 minutes for the theatrical release in 1984. It was restored to its original length on video and DVD.

Map: Page 152 **86**

"When love feels like magic, you call it destiny. When destiny has a sense of humor, you call it serendipity."

SERENDIPITY (2001)

Serendipity 3
225 East 60th Street

Jonathan (John Cusack) meets Sara (Kate Beckinsale) while buying the last pair of black cashmere gloves at Bloomingdale's. Jonathan gallantly allows Sara to buy them and she takes him out to Serendipity 3 for ice cream in thanks. They are quickly attracted to each other and then go ice skating at Wollman Rink in Central Park, thus beginning a game of fate.

Map: Page 114 ⑪

"It's my heart, and it's broken."

GREAT EXPECTATIONS (1998)

Tompkins Square Park

This movie is a modernized version of Charles Dickens's novel that moves the setting from 1810–20s London to 1990s New York. Finn Bell, a 10-year-old boy living in a Florida fishing village, falls in love with the beautiful Estella, a nice of the rich Ms. Dinsmoor, who gave him a surprise kiss while drinking water from fountain at her mansion. Seven years later, Finn (Ethan Hawke) makes the move to New York and begins his new life, struggling to become a successful artist. With just 10 weeks to complete the necessary paintings for his first gallery show, Finn begins drawing at the East Village's Tompkins Square Park, where he again encounters Estella (Gwyneth Paltrow), once again re-creating the water-fountain kiss of their childhood.

Map: Page 142 **70**

As Good As It Gets (1997)

Ardea
31-33 West 12th Street

A misanthropic, obsessive-compulsive novelist, Melvin (Jack Nicholson), and a gay artist, Simon (Greg Kinnear), live in the 1895-built, Beaux-Arts Ardea apartment building on 12th Street between Fifth and Sixth avenues. The film shows the Greenwich Village neighborhood when Melvin walks Simon's dog, Verdell. Melvin finds himself attracted to Carol (Helen Hunt), the only waitress who can tolerate him. What woman does not want to hear the compliment, "You make me want to be a better man"?

Map: Page 136 **63**

"That's incredible. Imagine seven million people all wanting to live together. Yeah, New York must be the friendliest place on earth."

CROCODILE DUNDEE (1986)

Columbus Circle Subway Station

The music swells as reporter Sue (Linda Kozlowski) takes off her shoes and runs down to the platform of the Columbus Circle subway station to find her former subject Mick Dundee (Paul Hogan) standing far beyond the crowd. Calling out to Sue, "I'm coming through," Dundee walks on heads of the cheering crowds to reach his beloved. In a case of life imitating art, Linda Kozlowski and Paul Hogan actually married after the movie. This memorable final-scene love confession was actually filmed on the same abandoned platform of Brooklyn's Hoyt–Schermerhorn subway station as Michael Jackson's "Bad".

Map: Page 130 **48**

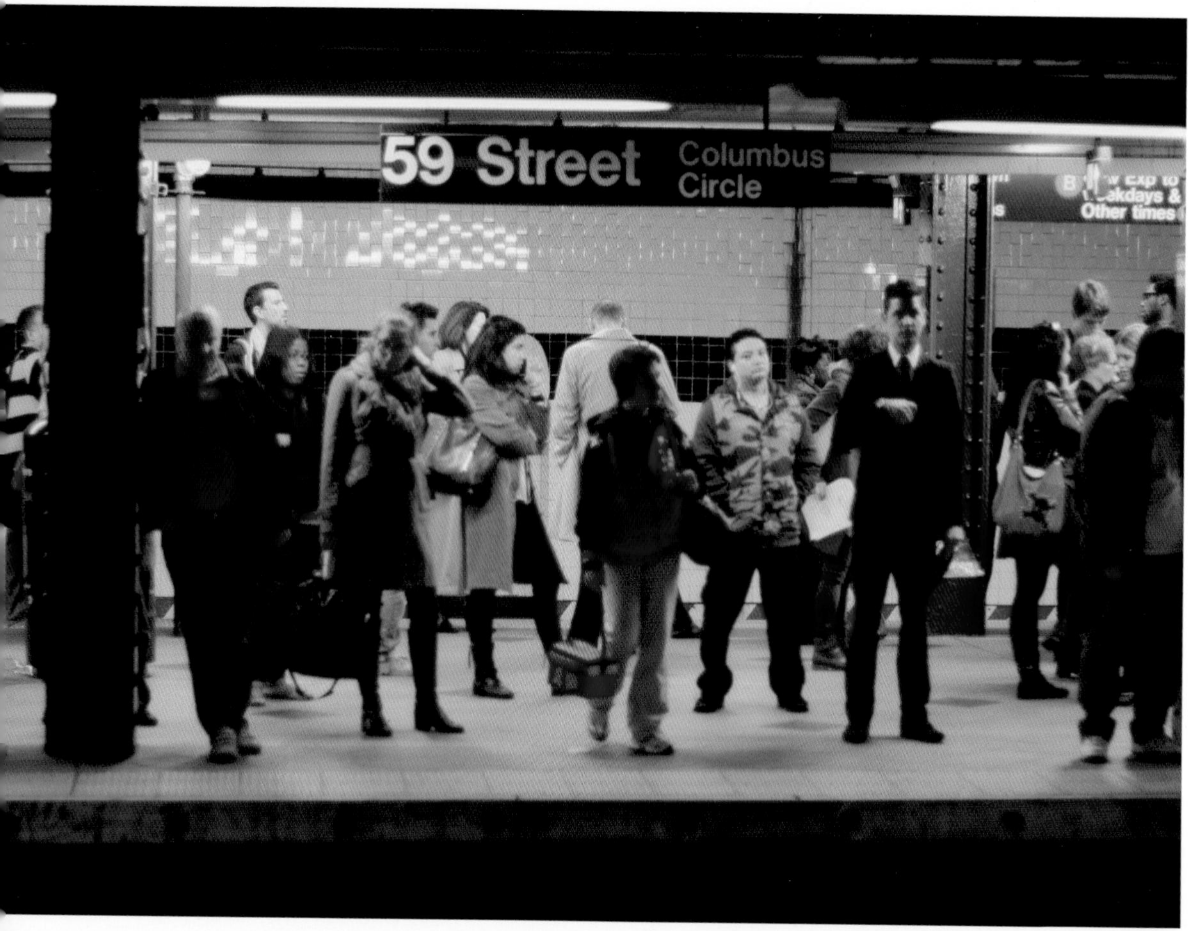
59 Street
Columbus
Circle
Other times

GHOSTBUSTERS (1984)

Hook & Ladder Company 8
14 North Moore Street

Fired from their job researching the paranormal at Columbia University, oddball scientists Peter (Bill Murray), Raymond (Dan Aykroyd), and Egon (Harold Ramis) set up a supernatural extermination service in a retired firehouse. While they face some skeptics at first, before long the Ghostbusters are the most in-demand service in town. Since the real-life Hook & Ladder Company 8 is an active firehouse, interior scenes were filmed at Fire Station No. 23 in Downtown Los Angeles. The New York firehouse is still in use, and if you pass by you can still see the sign from the film hanging up inside, as well as a Ghostbusters badge painted on the sidewalk.

Map: Page 148 **82**

"With great power comes great responsibility."

Spider-Man (2002)

Roosevelt Island Tramway at the Queensboro Bridge

Although created by computer imagery, the climax scene where the Green Goblin (Willem Dafoe) fights with Spider-Man (Tobey Maguire) at the Queensboro Bridge is an iconic New York City movie moment. The Goblin forces Spider-Man to choose whom he wants to save, and drops Mary Jane Watson (Kirsten Dunst) and a tramcar full of children. Of course our super hero, the friendly neighborhood Spider-Man, manages to save both of them. The tramway was upgraded in 2010. You can take a ride on it and take in a beautiful view of Manhattan for the cost of a subway ride.

Map: Page 114 **10**

"I am not going to New York to meet some woman who could be a crazy, sick lunatic! Didn't you see Fatal Attraction?"

SLEEPLESS IN SEATTLE (1993)

Empire State Building
34th Street and Fifth Avenue

The movie is inspired by *An Affair to Remember* (1957), which is considered one of the most romantic films of all time according to the American Film Institute. Although Cary Grant and Deborah Kerr never met on the top of the Empire State Building in the original, Sam (Tom Hanks) and Annie (Meg Ryan) did make it there on Valentine's Day, with the help of Sam's son Jonah (Ross Malinger) in the film's final scene. You can recreate the scene yourself with a visit to the skyscraper's observation deck, 1,250 feet above the city.

Map: Page 118 **32**

"Whoo-ah!"

SCENT OF A WOMAN (1992)

The Pierre Hotel
2 East 61st Street

A blind, retired army officer, Slade (Al Pacino), comes to New York with a prep school student, Charlie (Chris O'Donnell), who accepts a temporary job over Thanksgiving weekend to look after Slade. While waiting for drinks at an opulent hotel, Slade is captivated by Donna (Gabrielle Anwar), a beautiful young woman waiting for a date, because of the scent of her Ogilvie Sisters soap. A moment later, Slade leads her in a spectacular tango on the dance floor, surprising Charlie and everyone in the ballroom with his gracefulness. The tango scene was filmed at the grand ballroom of the Pierre Hotel with two choreographers over four nights.

Map: Page 126 **34**

"We are going to sit in giant teacups and spin round and round in circles until we puke."

Uptown Girls (2003)

Coney Island, Brooklyn

The spoiled daughter of a dead rock star, Molly (Brittany Murphy), and the 8-year-old daughter of a busy executive, Ray (Dakota Fanning), both feel painfully alone in the world. When she loses her money, Molly is forced to take a job as Ray's babysitter, and though the carefree nanny and serious child don't get along at first, the two begin to bond. When Ray's comatose father dies, Molly finds the missing girl at the Coney Island boardwalk, riding a giant teacup. After Ray throws up, she slaps Molly and punches her, as if trying to let all her anger out. Molly hugs her and each discovers a true friend in the other.

Map: Page 156 **00**

*"That's one of the advantages of being an adult.
You get to act like a kid anytime you feel like it."*

One Fine Day (1996)

Circle Line Sightseeing Cruise
Pier 83 at West 42nd Street

When Maggie and Sammy miss
their school field trip on the Circle
Line at Pier 83, Maggie's divorced
dad, reporter Jack (George
Clooney), and Sammy's divorced
mom, architect Melanie (Michelle
Pfeiffer), are forced to supervise
each other's kids for the day. As
they balance the demands of their
careers and children, Jack and Melanie run around the
city. After such a hectic day, is it any surprise that the two
quickly fall asleep on the couch at Melanie's house?

Map: Page 118 **31**

"You know, Herbert Hoover once stayed here on this floor."
"The vacuum guy?"

Home Alone 2:
Lost in New York (1992)

The Plaza Hotel
768 Fifth Avenue

In the rush to get to O'Hare Airport on time for a holiday vacation, 10-year-old Kevin (Macaulay Culkin) mistakenly gets on a flight to New York City—which the rest of his family doesn't realize until after they land in Miami. While his family panics, Kevin decides to enjoy Christmas vacation alone in New York. Using his Talkboy cassette recorder and his father's credit card, Kevin succeeds in checking into the luxurious Plaza Hotel. There he ends up spending $967 on room service, ordering chocolate cake, chocolate mousse, ice cream, and strawberry tarts…yum!

Map: Page 118 **23**

"Leave you at the flea market with this stupid costume jewelry!"

ETERNAL SUNSHINE OF THE SPOTLESS MIND (2004)

Orchard Street and Rivington Street

Joel (Jim Carrey) and Clementine (Kate Winslet) have been in turbulent relationship for two years. One day while together at a flea market on Orchard Street on the Lower East Side they get into an argument about having a baby. After a nasty breakup each decides to have the other erased from their memories, only to meet again unknowingly in a diner in Montauk. They then rekindle their relationship on the Long Island Railroad, in scenes shot on a real, moving train.

Map: Page 142 **73**

MOONSTRUCK (1987)

Lincoln Center
63rd Street and Columbus
Avenue

One full moon night, Loretta (Cher), a newly engaged Italian-American widow, sets out to share the news with her fiancé's estranged brother Ronny (Nicolas Cage). After a long, passionate conversation, the two sleep together. Although she feels ashamed the following morning, Loretta agrees to go to the opera with him that night, provided they never see each other again. She stops at church for confession, goes to a beauty salon to get her hair done and buys a new dress and shoes. Transformed, Loretta and Ronny meet at the fountain at Lincoln Center and she enjoys her first opera, *La Bohème*. Not long after Loretta's fiancé returns from visiting his mother in Italy, they all end up toasting her engagement to Ronny. *"Alla famiglia!"*

Map: Page 130 **50**

"Is life always this hard, or is it just when you're a kid?"

LÉON: THE PROFESSIONAL (1994)

Seventh Avenue and 58th Street

Although Luc Besson wrote the script for *Léon* in only 30 days, while waiting for the delayed shooting of *The Fifth Element*, this film is considered one of the best New York movies. From interior scenes shot inside the Chelsea Hotel, to the street where Léon (Jean Reno) and Mathilda (played by a 12-year-old Natalie Portman in her film debut) carry a houseplant as they move from one hotel to another, the film captures the gritty essence of 1990s New York—even though many interiors where shot on a Paris sound stage.

Map: Page 118 **29**

AUGUST RUSH (2007)

Washington Square Park

On a rooftop terrace looking down on Washington Square Park, cellist Lyla (Keri Russell) and guitarist Louis (Jonathan Rhys Meyers) share an enchanted night together under a full moon, but go their separate ways. They have a son together, whom Louis doesn't know about and whom Lyla believes died in an accident. Eleven years later, the boy, Evan (Freddie Highmore), runs away from the orphanage where he was raised to New York City, in hopes of discovering his roots. A child prodigy, he starts playing guitar as a street performer in the same park where his musician parents first met. It's music that finally brings them back together.

Map: Page 136 66

"Do you want to dance? Or do you want to dance?"

THE THOMAS CROWN AFFAIR (1999)

The Metropolitan Museum of Art
Fifth Avenue and 82nd Street

A bored billionaire, Thomas Crown (Pierce Brosnan), orchestrates an elaborate heist to steal a painting by Claude Monet from the Metropolitan Museum of Art. While insurance investigator Catherine (Rene Russo) suspects and chases Crown, she gets deeply involved with him. Crown decides to return the painting under the eyes of Catherine and dozens of police officers to prove his sincerity and test her loyalty to him. The painting at the center of the film, *San Giorgio Maggiore at Dusk*, is actually owned by The National Museum and Art Gallery, Cardiff, Wales. Although the exterior of the museum was portrayed by the Met, interior scenes were filmed at the New York Public Library and on a soundstage.

Map: Page 126 **39**

"Desperately Seeking Susan, Keep the faith, Tuesday 10 a.m. Battery Park Gangway 1."

DESPERATELY SEEKING SUSAN (1986)

Battery Park

Roberta (Rosanna Arquette), a bored suburban housewife in New Jersey, becomes fascinated by a stranger named Susan (Madonna) after reading messages of love in the personal ads section of a New York tabloid paper. Following an ad from the paper, Roberta goes to Battery Park to peek at their rendezvous. Later, Roberta tries to meet her at the park again and accidentally gets hit on the head. She wakes up with amnesia, and is mistaken for Susan. The film was released early in Madonna's rise to popularity, and includes her hit song "Into the Groove" during the Danceteria scene.

Map: Page 152 **95**

"Well I mean, I could dance with you, but you're not my dream girl or nothing like that…"

SATURDAY NIGHT FEVER (1977)

86th Street, Bensonhurst, Brooklyn

Saturday Night Fever opens with an aerial shot from the Brooklyn Bridge to the neighborhood of Bay Ridge in Brooklyn, emphasizing its distance from Manhattan. Then 18-year-old Brooklyn native Tony Manero (John Travolta) appears, strolling down 86th Street to the Bee Gees' song, "Stayin' Alive". He buys two slices of pizza at Lenny's Pizza and keeps on walking. The film was based on a 1976 story from *New York* magazine, though the author later admitted it was fabricated. The huge commercial success of this movie significantly helped to popularize disco music around the world and, of course, John Travolta.

Map: Page 156 **99**

THE GODFATHER PART II (1974)

6th Street between Avenues A & B

In 1917, Vito Corleone (Robert De Niro) lives in a tenement with his wife and son and works at a grocery store as an honest clerk. Three years later he shoots and kills Don Fanucci (Gastone Moschin) during the festival of San Gennaro and begins to become the respected and feared Don Corleone. It took six months to transform East 6th Street into the Little Italy of 1917—including installation of new fronts and signs, re-painting buildings, and changing lampposts. The grocery store where Vito works and Don Fanucci's apartment are set at 523 and 538 East 6th Street.

Map: Page 142 **71**

"Finance is a gun. Politics is knowing when to pull the trigger."

THE GODFATHER PART III (1990)

Elizabeth Street between Prince and East Houston Streets

Much of *The Godfather Trilogy* takes place in the historic Little Italy neighborhood, on the streets around Saint Patrick's Old Cathedral. It is here, on Elizabeth Street, that Vincent Mancini (Andy Garcia) kills enemy mob boss Zasa, while disguised as a policeman. Though the street is now part of trendy NoLIta (short for north of Little Italy) and lined with cafés and boutiques, you can still feel the atmosphere from the film with a short walk to the center of Little Italy: Mulberry Street between Broome and Grand streets. Visit in September to experience the annual feast of San Gennaro, when vendors line the street.

Map: Page 142 **76**

"You know what I wish I had right now?"
"No, what?"
"Razzles."

13 GOING ON 30 (2004)

Empire–Fulton Ferry Park
Brooklyn

After a prank is played on her at her 13th birthday party, Jenna (Jennifer Garner) wakes up to discover she is a successful fashion magazine editor with a Fifth Avenue apartment. She tracks down her one-time best friend Matt (Mark Ruffalo), a struggling photographer, who she mistakenly blamed for the prank 17 years earlier, and together they work on a magazine project. One night they buy Razzles candy, Jenna's favorite, and take a walk in the park after checking photos for the project. With a beautiful nighttime view of Manhattan and the Brooklyn Bridge they become closer again and kiss.

Map: Page 152 **87**

"All you need is love."

ACROSS THE UNIVERSE (2007)

Rooftop at ABC Carpet Building
19th Street and Broadway

Julie Taymor's fantasy musical movie featuring 33 Beatles' classics tells the story of the love affair between Jude (Jim Sturgess), a Liverpool dockworker, and Lucy (Evan Rachel Wood), a girl from upper-crust East Coast suburbia, set amid the counterculture of 1960s politics, sex, drugs, and rock 'n' roll. The memorable last scene, which recalls the Beatles' famous rooftop concert, was shot on the roof of the ABC Carpet & Home building on Ladies' Mile; the street scene below was shot in TriBeCa at Desbrosses and Greenwich streets. The scene includes the iconic songs "Hey Jude", "Don't Let Me Down", "All You Need is Love", and the finale, "Lucy in the Sky with Diamonds."

Map: Page 136 **61**

Desbrosses and Greenwich Streets

"I'm new here in town. Just in from Texas, you know…and I'm looking for the Statue of Liberty."

MIDNIGHT COWBOY (1969)

Park Avenue and 68th Street

Joe Buck (John Voight) arrives in New York from Texas in hopes of making it big as a gigolo. He begins wandering the city streets dressed like a rodeo cowboy and looking for women to hustle. On Park Avenue on the Upper East Side, he asks a wealthy-looking lady for directions to the Statue of Liberty, but his attempt to pick her up fails. When he is finally successful in bedding a middle-aged woman, Cass (Sylvia Miles), she cons him into giving her $20 instead. Later he meets the equally hard-on-his-luck "Ratso" Rizzo (Dustin Hoffman) at a bar. Crossing 58th Street and Sixth Avenue, Rizzo lets out his famous cry: "I'm walkin' here! I'm walkin' here!" It's still debated whether the line was improvised or scripted.

Map: Page 126 36

"Mrs. Dalloway said she would buy the flowers herself."

THE HOURS (2002)

Hudson Street and 14th Street
Meatpacking District

This acclaimed film explores the effect of Virginia Woolf's 1925 novel *Mrs. Dalloway* on three women of three different generations. One beautiful morning in the present day, editor Clarissa (Meryl Streep) visits the Meatpacking District loft of her longtime friend and former lover, the poet Richard (Ed Harris). She carries a bundle of flowers to cheer him up, and to convince him to attend his lifetime achievement award ceremony and party that evening. When she comes to pick him up for the ceremony in the afternoon, Richard, who is dying from AIDS, throws himself out of the window of his top-floor apartment, committing suicide.

Map: Page 136 **68**

"Good Lord, it still stands. The world has changed all around it, but Roebling's erection still stands!"

KATE & LEOPOLD (2001)

Brooklyn Bridge

The movie starts with a scene of the Brooklyn Bridge under construction. The Brooklyn Bridge was completed in 1883 as the longest suspension bridge in the world, thanks to the efforts of the Roebling family. Leopold (Hugh Jackman), a duke who travels through time from 1876 New York to the 21st century, falls in love with Kate (Meg Ryan), a career woman in modern New York. When she discovers her time-traveling beau's secret, Kate decides to chase Leopold through a time window that opens at the Brooklyn Bridge.

Map: Page 152 **84**

30 ROCK (2006–2013)

30 Rockefeller Plaza

In the very first episode of *30 Rock*, Liz (Tina Fey), head writer of *The Girlie Show*, buys all the hot dogs from a street vendor to hinder a man who tries to cheat the line. She then walks through the famous Rockefeller Plaza to her office and studio, where she encounters all the actors, writers, and executives that make her job difficult—and hilarious. The comedy show was based on Fey's experiences as head writer for *Saturday Night Live*, which is also filmed at 30 Rockefeller Plaza, a.k.a. 30 Rock.

Map: Page 118　**17**

"My job is not to look after you, it's to look after the man who's been threatened, if there was a threat. My job, as it concerns you, is to investigate you."

THE INTERPRETER (2005)

United Nations, General Assembly

Sydney Pollack's final movie was the first ever filmed inside of the United Nations—and it took a direct appeal from the director to then U.N. Secretary-General Kofi Annan to get permission to film there. In the film, Nicole Kidman stars as Silvia, an interpreter at the General Assembly who is forced to become involved in a plan to assassinate the president of the African nation of Matobo. The nearby Dag Hammarskjöld Plaza is named for the organization's second Secretary-General, who died in a mysterious plane crash while mediating Congo's independence—perhaps the most famous real-life case of intrigue involving the U.N. and Africa. Guided tours of the United Nations are available Monday through Friday.

Map: Page 114 **5**

"Oh, do you feel the breeze from the subway. Isn't it delicious?"

THE SEVEN YEAR ITCH (1955)

Lexington Avenue between 51st and 52nd Streets

Having just seen *Creature from the Black Lagoon*, an un-named girl (Marilyn Monroe) and Richard (Tom Ewell) come out from the Trans-Lux Theatre on a hot summer's day. She stands over a subway gate as the breeze from the train blows her white dress up around her legs. The scene was filmed on location early on the morning of September 15, 1954, with thousands of excited fans crowded nearby. A second take was shot on a sound stage at the 20th Century Fox lot. While the image of Monroe with her dress billowing around her is one of the most iconic images of the 20th century, the film actually only shows her legs cut with reaction shots, never in full-length like the famous image.

Map: Page 114 **8**

FILM AND TV LOCATIONS

New York City's Top 100 **Locations:**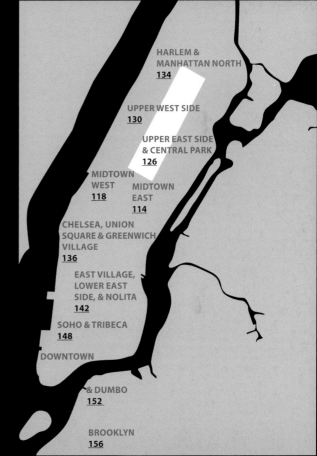

+

20 Restaurant & Bar **Locations:**

+

Top 33 Sex and the City **Locations:**

+

9 SMASH **Broadway Locations:**

MIDTOWN EAST

1. THE FISHER KING (1991)
Grand Central Terminal
While Parry follows Lydia, the commuters start waltzing in the main hall

2. MEN IN BLACK 3 (2012)
The Chrysler Building
In order to save Agent K, J jumps from the building to travel back to 1969

3. SUPERMAN (1978)
The Daily Planet: 220 East 42nd Street
Clark Kent becomes a reporter at the *Daily Planet* in Metropolis

4. SCARFACE (1983)
Tudor City
Tony tries to assassinate a Bolivian journalist by planting a bomb in the journalist's car

5. THE INTERPRETER (2005)
The United Nations, General Assembly
Silvia is forced to be involved in the plan to assassinate the president of Matobo

6. MAN ON A LEDGE (2012)
The Roosevelt Hotel
Nick climbs on the ledge from his room on the 21st floor and threatens to jump

7. SERENDIPITY (2001)
The Waldorf Astoria Hotel
Sara and Jonathan test their fate in the elevators at the hotel

8. THE SEVEN YEAR ITCH (1955)
Lexington Avenue between 51st & 52nd Streets
Marilyn Monroe stands on the subway grate and her white dress is blown up showing her famous legs

9. MANHATTAN (1979)
58th Street & The East River, Sutton Place
Isaac and Mary chat until sunrise at the East River

10. SPIDER-MAN (2002)
Roosevelt Island Tramway at the Queensboro Bridge
Green Goblin forces Spider-Man to choose between saving Mary Jane or a tramcar full of children

⑪ SERENDIPITY (2001)
Serendipity 3
Sara takes Jonathan out to Serendipity 3 for ice cream to thank him

⑫ SPLASH (1984)
Bloomingdale's
Madison shops for clothes and picks up English from watching television at the department store

⑬ BIG (1988)
FAO Schwarz: 767 Fifth Avenue
Josh and Mr. MacMillan play "Heart and Soul" and "Chopsticks" by dancing on the keys of a giant piano

⑭ BREAKFAST AT TIFFANY'S (1961)
Tiffany & Co.: 727 Fifth Avenue
Holly eats a pastry and drinks coffee while window-shopping in her famous little black dress

① THE DEVIL WEARS PRADA (2006)
Smith & Wollensky: 797 Third Avenue
Andy runs to get Miranda a steak for lunch

② BASQUIAT (1996)
Mr. Chow: 324 East 57th Street
Basquiat dines with Andy Warhol after his opening

③ COCKTAIL (1988)
Baker Street: 1152 First Avenue
Brian starts working as a bartender at the bar

① SEX AND THE CITY (1998–2004)
Monkey Bar: 60 East 54th Street
Carrie and Mr. Big come to see a jazz show while trying to become friends

② SEX AND THE CITY (1998–2004)
Tao: 42 East 58th Street
Mr. Big shows up with a supermodel, while Carrie is dating the jazz musician Ray

Central Park

54th Street
52nd Street
57th Street
59th Street
49th Street
47th Street
44th Street
42nd Street
34th Street

Eleventh Avenue
Tenth Avenue
Ninth Avenue
Eighth Avenue
Seventh Avenue
Broadway
Sixth Avenue
Avenue of the Americas
Fifth Avenue
Madison Avenue
Park Avenue
Lexington Avenue
Third Avenue

MIDTOWN WEST

⑮ LETTERS TO JULIET (2010)
Bryant Park
Sophie receives an invitation from Claire and Lorenzo and decides to attend their wedding

⑯ 9 ½ WEEKS (1986)
The Algonquin Hotel
Wearing a man's suit, hat, and fake mustache, Elizabeth appears in the lobby bar in the hotel

⑰ 30 ROCK (2006–2013)
30 Rockefeller Plaza
Home to the office and studio of Liz and *The Girlie Show*

⑱ THE ADJUSTMENT BUREAU (2012)
Top of the Rock: 45 Rockefeller Plaza
David and Elise find themselves trapped and surrounded on the observation deck

⑲ SOMETHING'S GOTTA GIVE (2003)
Christie's
Erica's daughter Marin works as an auctioneer

⑳ THE DEVIL WEARS PRADA (2006)
1221 The Avenue of Americas
Andy works as a junior personal assistant to Miranda at *Runway Magazine*

㉑ ANNIE (1982)
Radio City Music Hall
Annie and Daddy Warbucks have a private screening of a film

㉒ MANHATTAN (1979)
Museum of Modern Art
Isaac runs into Mary at an Equal Rights Amendment fund-raising event at the museum

㉓ HOME ALONE 2: LOST IN NEW YORK (1992)
The Plaza Hotel
Kevin succeeds in checking in the hotel by using his Talkboy tape recorder and his father's credit card

㉔ MIDNIGHT COWBOY (1969)
Sixth Avenue and 58th Street
Ratso shouts "I'm walkin' here" to a passing cabbie who nearly hits him with his car

㉕ VANILLA SKY (2001)
Times Square
David drives his black Porsche to the empty square

㉖ FAME (1980)
46th Street between Sixth and Seventh Avenues
Students of the School of Performing Arts dance in the street, holding up traffic

㉗ TAXI DRIVER (1976)
Eighth Avenue and 47th Street
Travis walks down Eighth Avenue after work in the morning

㉘ SEINFELD (1989–1998)
Soup Nazi (The Original Soup Man)
Jerry, George, and Elaine go to a new soup stand where the owner is referred to as the Soup Nazi

㉙ LÉON: THE PROFESSIONAL (1994)
Seventh Avenue and 58th Street
Léon and Mathilda carry a houseplant in hand as they move from one hotel to another

㉚ TOOTSIE (1982)
Theater Row
Michael confesses, "I was a better man with you as a woman than I ever was with a woman as a man"

㉛ ONE FINE DAY (1996)
Circle Line Sightseeing Cruise
Maggie and Sammy miss their school field trip at Pier 83 for the Circle Line

㉜ SLEEPLESS IN SEATTLE (1993)
Empire State Building
Sam and Annie meet on the observation deck with Jonah's help on Valentine's Day

㉝ HOW TO LOSE A GUY IN 10 DAYS (2003)
Madison Square Garden
Ben and Andie go to see a New York Knicks basketball game

④ WALL STREET (1987)
21 Club: 21 West 52nd Street
Gordon Gekko treats Bud to steak tartare for lunch

⑤ **NEW YEAR'S EVE (2011)**
Stardust Diner: 1650 Broadway

After midnight on New Year's Eve, teen Hailey meets her mother, Kim, at the diner before heading to an after-party

⑥ **ONE FINE DAY (1996)**
Carnegie Deli: 854 Seventh Avenue

Maggie and Melanie use the bathroom on the way to a soccer game

❸ **SEX AND THE CITY: THE MOVIE (2008)**
New York Public Library

Mr. Big's fear of marriage devastates Carrie, and she flees the wedding at the library

❹ **SEX AND THE CITY (1998–2004)**
Manolo Blahnik: 31 West 54th Street

Carrie claims to be able to run a marathon in her favorite shoes

❺ **SEX AND THE CITY: THE MOVIE 2 (2010)**
Bergdorf Goodman: 754 Fifth Avenue

The girls meet at the entrance of the store and buy wedding gifts for Anthony and Stanford

❻ **SEX AND THE CITY: THE MOVIE 2 (2010)**
Ziegfeld Theatre: 141 West 54th Street

Miley Cyrus shares an air kiss with Samantha wearing the same dress at a movie premiere

❼ **SEX AND THE CITY (1998–2004)**
Russian Samovar: 256 West 52nd Street

Carrie has a first date with the mysterious artist Aleksandr Petrovsky at the classic Russian restaurant

❽ **SEX AND THE CITY (1998–2004)**
Da Marino Restaurant: 220 West 49th Street

Mr. Big serenades Carrie in their second go-round

SMASH
BROADWAY
LOCATIONS

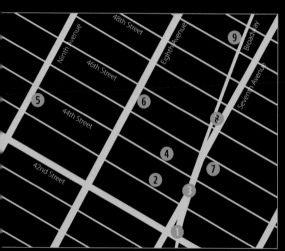

1. Times Square subway entrance that Karen takes 2. 229 West 43rd Steet.: dance studio 3. Times Square and 44th Street.: Tom and Ivy have lunch 4. Shubert Theatre: home to the show, *Heaven on Earth* 5. Westway Diner: Julia and Michael share a sweet 6. Townhouses appear when Karen and Ivy head to the audition 7. Bond 45: Eileen throws a martini in Jerry's face 8. Times Square and 46th Street.: drunk Ivy and Karen perform with street

UPPER EAST SIDE & CENTRAL PARK

34 **SCENT OF A WOMAN** (1992)
The Pierre Hotel
Slade leads Donna in a spectacular tango on the
dance floor of the grand ballroom

35 **ANNIE HALL** (1977)
Annie Hall's Apartment
Annie finds a parking spot on 68th Street near her
apartment

36 **MIDNIGHT COWBOY** (1969)
Park Avenue and 68th Street
Joe looks for wealthy women to become his
customers on Park Avenue

37 **BREAKFAST AT TIFFANY'S** (1961)
Holly's Apartment: 169 East 71st Street
One morning Holly is awakened by new tenant
Paul Varjak ringing the doorbell

38 **CRUEL INTENTIONS** (1999)
Valmont Mansion: 2 East 79th Street
Kathryn and her step-brother Sebastian live in the
Harry F. Sinclair mansion

39 **THE THOMAS CROWN AFFAIR** (1999)
The Metropolitan Museum of Art
Crown orchestrates an elaborate heist and steals a
painting from the museum

40 **MEN IN BLACK** (1997)
Guggenheim Museum
New York police officer Edwards chases an alien
on the rooftop of the museum

41 **DEFINITELY, MAYBE** (2007)
The Pond, Central Park
Emily confesses to Will that she slept with his
roommate

42 **MADAGASCAR** (2005)
Central Park Zoo, Central Park
Alex, Marty, Melman, and Gloria leave the zoo and
get shipwrecked on the island of Madagascar

43 **LOVE STORY** (1970)
Wollman Rink, Central Park
Oliver and Jennifer spend a happy day together as he
ice skates and she watches from the bleachers

44 KRAMER VS. KRAMER (1979)
The Mall, Central Park
Billy tries to ride a bicycle for the first time with help from his father Ted

45 IT COULD HAPPEN TO YOU (1994)
Bethesda Terrace, Central Park
Yvonne and Charlie enjoy rollerblading here before he plunges into the pond

46 UPTOWN GIRLS (2003)
Bow Bridge, Central Park
Molly attempts suicide by jumping off a bridge but finds a mere four feet of water in the lake

47 WALL STREET (1987)
Sheep Meadow, Central Park
Bud meets Gekko to record evidence of his insider trading

9 SEX AND THE CITY: THE MOVIE (2008)
Lumi: 963 Lexington Avenue
A pregnant Charlotte bumps into Mr. Big at a restaurant after he fails to show up at the wedding

10 SEX AND THE CITY (1998–2004)
The Boathouse Restaurant: Central Park
Mr. Big and Carrie meet for lunch and end up in the pond

11 SEX AND THE CITY: THE MOVIE (2008)
1030 Fifth Avenue
Carrie and Big live in a "little more down to earth" apartment on the 12th floor

UPPER EAST SIDE

UPPER WEST SIDE

48 **GHOSTBUSTERS** (1984)
Columbus Circle
Gozer's destructor, the giant Marshmallow Man, approaches through the circle

CROCODILE DUNDEE (1986)
Columbus Circle Subway Station
Sue and Mick exchange love messages through the crowd while waiting for a train

49 **GHOSTBUSTERS** (1984)
Gozer's Building: 15 Central Park West
Dana and Louis live in the building built as a gateway to summon the ancient and evil Gozer

50 **MOONSTRUCK** (1987)
Lincoln Center
Loretta and Ronny meet at the fountain of Lincoln Center to see the opera *La Bohème*

51 **DIE HARD WITH A VENGEANCE** (1995)
72nd Street Subway Station
McClane and Carver are instructed by Simon to travel to Wall Street station within 30 minutes

52 **SINGLE WHITE FEMALE** (1992)
The Ansonia: 2109 Broadway
Allie looks for a roommate after separating from her boyfriend and settles on Hedra

53 **ROSEMARY'S BABY** (1968)
The Dakota: 1 West 72nd Street
Rosemary and Guy move into an antiquated New York apartment building with mysterious neighbors

54 **NIGHT AT THE MUSEUM** (2006)
American Museum of Natural History
Larry takes a job as a night watchman at the museum

55 **YOU'VE GOT MAIL** (1998)
Zabar's
Kathleen goes shopping and mistakenly stands in a cash-only line at the gourmet food store

7 **THE FIRST WIVES CLUB** (1996)
Leopard at des Artistes: 1 West 67th Street
Brenda, Elise, and Annie have lunch together and discuss their failed marriages

⑧ **WHEN HARRY MET SALLY... (1989)**
Cafe Luxembourg: 200 West 70th Street
Marie mentions that "restaurants are to people in
the '80s what theater was to people in the '60s"

⑨ **YOU'VE GOT MAIL (1998)**
Café Lalo: 201 West 83rd Street
"NY152" (Joe) asks "Shopgirl" (Kathleen) to meet at
the café

⑫ **SEX AND THE CITY: THE MOVIE 2 (2010)**
Empire Hotel: 44 West 63rd Street
Carrie catches her husband flirting with Carmen,
a banker, at a bar

⑬ **SEX AND THE CITY (1998–2004)**
Columbus Circle Fountains
Carrie and Aidan realize their relationship is not
going to work at the picturesque fountain

UPPER WEST SIDE

56 **SPIDER-MAN** (2002)
Columbia University
Peter is bitten on the hand by a super spider at a
genetics laboratory

57 **MALCOLM X** (1992)
Apollo Theater: 253 West 125th Street
Malcolm X gives a speech in front of the iconic
Harlem theater

58 **THE ROYAL TENENBAUMS** (2001)
The Tenenbaum House: 444 West 144th Street
At Henry and Etheline's wedding, Eli crashes his car
into the side of the house

10 **SEINFELD** (1989–1998)
Monk's Café (Tom's Restaurant): 2880 Broadway
The restaurant serves Jerry's egg-white omelet and
Elaine's Big Salad

CHELSEA, UNION SQUARE, & GREENWICH VILLAGE

59 SID AND NANCY (1986)
Hotel Chelsea
Sid and Nancy fight in a drug-induced haze, and he stabs her in the hotel room

60 SPIDER-MAN (2002)
The Daily Bugle: Flatiron Building
Upon graduating from school, Peter works as a freelance photographer for the newspaper

61 ACROSS THE UNIVERSE (2007)
Rooftop of ABC Carpet Building
Sadie, Jojo, and Jude play "Don't Let Me Down" and "All You Need is Love"

62 THE AGE OF INNOCENCE (1993)
The Beaufort's House : National Arts Club
Mrs. Beaufort always hosts a ball on an opera night at her grand home

63 AS GOOD AS IT GETS (1997)
Ardea: 31–33 West 12th Street
Melvin and Simon live in the 1895 Beaux-Arts apartment building on West 12th Street

64 PRIME (2005)
Village Cinema
While standing in line at the cinema, Rafi is introduced to David

65 I AM LEGEND (2007)
Neville's Townhouse: 11 Washington Square
Neville lives in a heavily fortified townhouse with a laboratory in the basement

66 AUGUST RUSH (2007)
Washington Square Park
August meets Louis at the park and they play guitar together without knowing they are blood relatives

67 FRIENDS (1994-2004)
The Friends Apartment: 90 Bedford Street
Monica's purple-walled apartment is the main stage of the show

68 THE HOURS (2002)
Hudson Street and 14th Street
Clarissa visits Richard's loft in the Meatpacking District carrying a bundle of flowers

CHELSEA

⑪ **MAN ON A LEDGE (2012)**
Old Town Bar: 45 East 18th Street
Nick meets Joey, Angie, and Lydia, and introduces
Lydia to the hotel concierge, who is Nick's father

⑫ **NEXT STOP, GREENWICH VILLAGE (1976)**
Caffe Reggio: 119 MacDougal Street
Larry, Sarah and his friends regularly gather here

⑭ **SEX AND THE CITY (1998–2004)**
Church of the Transfiguration: 1 East 29th Street
The "Little Church Around the Corner", where
Samantha meets "the Friar"

⑮ **SEX AND THE CITY (1998–2004)**
Eleven Madison Park: 11 Madison Avenue
Mr. Big tells Carrie that he is engaged to another
woman at this upscale restaurant

⑯ **SEX AND THE CITY (1998–2004)**
City Bakery: 3 West 18th Street
Carrie and Samantha discuss "the face girl" over
lunch

⑰ **SEX AND THE CITY (1998–2004)**
Pete's Tavern: 129 East 18th Street
Miranda asks Steve to marry her

⑱ **SEX AND THE CITY (1998–2004)**
Il Cantinori: 32 East 10th Street
Carrie celebrates her 35th birthday all by herself

⑲ **SEX AND THE CITY (1998–2004)**
Gray's Papaya: 402 Sixth Avenue
Carrie stops at this takeout spot for a hot dog after
her book party

⑳ **SEX AND THE CITY (1998–2004)**
Jefferson Market Garden
Miranda and Steve get married at a community
garden where there was once a women's prison

㉑ **SEX AND THE CITY (1998–2004)**
The Pleasure Chest: 156 Seventh Avenue South
Charlotte buys herself a "Rabbit"

UNION SQUARE

㉒ SEX AND THE CITY (1998–2004)
Carrie's Apartment: 66 Perry Street
The steps where Carrie often perched are real,
although the fictional location is "245 E. 73rd St."

㉓ SEX AND THE CITY (1998–2004)
Magnolia Bakery: 401 Bleecker Street
To give up cigarettes for her new man Aidan, Carrie
turns to cake, and joins Miranda for cupcakes

㉔ SEX AND THE CITY (1998–2004)
Pastis: 9 Ninth Avenue
Carrie and "the Russian" have brunch here in the
heart of the Meatpacking District

㉕ SEX AND THE CITY: THE MOVIE (2008)
Diane von Furstenberg: 874 Washington Street
Carrie talks on her cell phone to Samantha about
her and Big's decision to get married

㉖ SEX AND THE CITY: THE MOVIE (2008)
Buddakan: 75 Ninth Avenue
Carrie and Big's rehearsal dinner for their wedding is
held here

EAST VILLAGE, LOWER EAST SIDE, & NOLITA

69 TAXI DRIVER (1976)
Iris' Brothel: 226 East 13th Street
Travis shoots to kill Sport and other men to save Iris

70 GREAT EXPECTATIONS (1998)
Tompkins Square Park
Finn encounters Estella again by re-creating the water-fountain kiss of their childhood

71 THE GODFATHER PART II (1974)
6th Street between Avenues A and B
Young Vito Corleone murders Don Fanucci during the feast of San Gennaro in Little Italy

72 WHEN HARRY MET SALLY... (1989)
Katz's Delicatessen: 205 East Houston Street
Sally fakes orgasm at the deli to prove her point as other customers watch

73 ETERNAL SUNSHINE OF THE SPOTLESS MIND (2004)
Orchard Street and Rivington Street
While together at a flea market, Clementine and Joel get into an argument about having a baby

74 ACROSS THE UNIVERSE (2007)
Rivington Street and Clinton Street
Jojo arrives in the 1960s East Village after his younger brother is killed in the Detroit riots

75 P.S. I LOVE YOU (2007)
Holly and Gerry's Apartment: 254 Broome Street
Holly and Gerry walk back to their apartment while arguing over an incident at dinner

76 THE GODFATHER PART III (1990)
Elizabeth Street between Prince and East Houston Streets
Vincent, disguised as a policeman, kills his enemy, the mafia boss Zasa, in the Little Italy

77 THE GODFATHER (1972)
Genco Pura Olive Oil Co.: 128 Mott Street
Vito is shot on the street in front of Genco Co. by Sollozzo's men and lands in the hospital

EAST VILLAGE

⑬ NICK AND NORAH'S INFINITE PLAYLIST (2008)
Veselka: 144 Second Avenue
Nick calls Norah, apologizing for leaving, and she meets him again at the diner

⑭ SMASH (2012–)
Café Orlin: 41 St. Marks Place
Karen waits tables at the cafe in the East Village while going to auditions

⑮ ONCE UPON A TIME IN AMERICA (1984)
McSorley's Old Ale House: 15 East 7th Street
The young gang members discuss whether to take the dollar to burn the newsstand or roll the drunk

⑯ CROCODILE DUNDEE (1986)
Vazak's Horseshoe Bar: 108 Avenue B
The taxi driver takes Mick to this bar to introduce New York "wildlife"

⑰ FRIENDS WITH BENEFITS (2011)
Café Habana: 17 Prince Street
Jamie and Dylan open up to each other while having lunch

⑱ NICK AND NORAH'S INFINITE PLAYLIST (2008)
Arlene's Grocery: 95 Stanton Street
Nora comes to see Nick's band The Jerk-Offs perform at the club

㉗ SEX AND THE CITY (1998–2004)
St. Mark's Comics: 11 St. Marks Place
Carrie meets Wade, a 30-something still living with his parents

㉘ SEX AND THE CITY (1998–2004)
Patricia Field Boutique: 306 Bowery
The show became famous for the fashion showcased by Patricia Field, the costume designer

EAST VILLAGE

ST. MARK'S COMICS

GROCERY
FAST DELIVERY

95. ARLENES GROCERY

SOHO & TRIBECA

78 **PRIME** (2005)
Dean and DeLuca: 560 Broadway
Rafi and David bump into each other at the SoHo gourmet store

79 **GHOST** (1990)
Sam and Molly's Loft: 102 Prince Street
Sam and Molly move into a cast-iron building in SoHo

80 **HITCH** (2005)
Greene Street and Spring Street
Hitch suddenly jumps on Sara's car to get back together with her

81 **TWO WEEK NOTICE** (2002)
Tribeca Grand Hotel
Lucy finds George and June playing strip chess at his hotel residence

82 **GHOSTBUSTERS** (1984)
Hook & Ladder Company 8
Walter releases hundreds of captured ghosts into the city from the headquarters' basement

19 **UNFAITHFUL** (2002)
Café Noir: 32 Grand Street
Connie and Paul make love passionately in the bathroom while her friends wait for her at the table

20 **DEFINITELY, MAYBE** (2008)
The Odeon: 145 West Broadway
Summer writes a piece on the man Will is working for and they start dating

29 **SEX AND THE CITY** (1998-2004)
Louis K. Meisel Gallery: 141 Prince Street
The gallery where Charlotte worked in SoHo

30 **SEX AND THE CITY: THE MOVIE 2** (2010)
Scavolini: 429 West Broadway
Samantha asks the girls to go with her to Abu Dhabi over lunch

31 **SEX AND THE CITY** (1998-2004)
Onieals: 174 Grand Street
"Scout", the bar owned by Steve and Aidan

DOWNTOWN & DUMBO

83 **ANGER MANAGEMENT (2003)**
New York County Supreme Court
Dave is found guilty of assault, and sentenced to
anger-management therapy

84 **KATE & LEOPOLD (2001)**
Brooklyn Bridge
Leopold follows Stuart and falls with him into a
temporal portal between centuries

85 **I AM LEGEND (2007)**
South Street Seaport
After Sam is attacked by infected dogs, Neville
seeks revenge against the "Darkseekers"

86 **ONCE UPON A TIME IN AMERICA (1984)**
Washington Street and Water Street, Brooklyn
Little Dominic is shot to death by Bugsy on the
street near the Manhattan Bridge

87 **13 GOING ON 30 (2004)**
Empire–Fulton Ferry Park, Brooklyn
After checking photos, Jenna and Matt take a
nighttime walk in the park and kiss

88 **HITCH (2005)**
North Cove Marina
Hitch meets Sara at the marina and takes her jet
skiing on the Hudson River

89 **DIE HARD WITH A VENGEANCE (1995)**
Federal Reserve Bank
Simon steals $140 billion in gold bullion from the
bank by a subway explosion

90 **NATIONAL TREASURE (2004)**
Trinity Church
Beneath the church Ben, Riley, Abigail, and Patrick
finally find the vast treasure trove

91 **INSIDE MAN (2006)**
Manhattan Trust Bank: 20 Exchange Place
Dalton and his company rob Manhattan Trust Bank
and take hostages

92 **KATE & LEOPOLD (2001)**
Leopold's House: 1 Hanover Square
Leopold finds his mother's ring in his hidden
drawer at his still-existing house

93 **HOW TO LOSE A GUY IN 10 DAYS (2003)**
Alexander Hamilton Custom House
At the company ball Andie and Ben sing a poor
version of "You Are So Vain" to humiliate each other

94 **MEN IN BLACK (1997)**
M.I.B. Headquaters
Edwards passes the test and becomes Agent J

95 **DESPERATELY SEEKING SUSAN (1985)**
Battery Park
Following an ad in a tabloid, Roberta goes to
Battery Park to peek at Susan's rendezvous

96 **SPLASH (1984)**
Liberty Island
A naked mermaid, Madison, sheds her fins and
arrives at Liberty Island

97 **HITCH (2005)**
Ellis Island
Hitch shows Sara her great-great grandfather's
entry in a ledger on Ellis Island

32 **SEX AND THE CITY (1998–2004)**
Century 21: 22 Cortlandt Street
Carrie enjoys bargain hunting downtown while she
is serving jury duty

33 **SEX AND THE CITY (1998–2004)**
Staten Island Ferry
Charlotte announces, "I'm getting married this year!"

DOWNTOWN

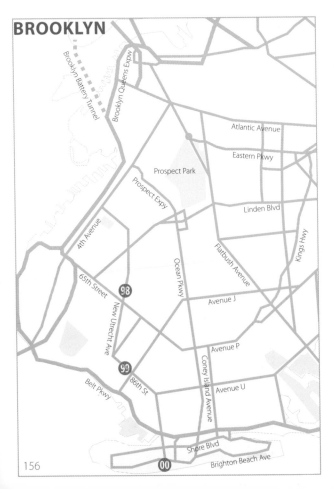

BROOKLYN

98 THE FRENCH CONNECTION (1971)
62nd Street and New Utrecht Ave Station
Nicoli escapes the hijacked train and Doyle shoots
him when he attempts to escape

99 SATURDAY NIGHT FEVER (1977)
86th Street, Bensonhurst
Tony strolls down 86th Street to the Bee Gees' song,
"Stayin' Alive"

00 UPTOWN GIRLS (2003)
Coney Island
When Ray's father dies, Molly finds Ray in Coney
Island riding a giant teacup

INDEX

Museyon Inc.
20 East 46th Street, New York, NY 10017
info@museyon.com

Publisher: Akira Chiba
Editors: Heather Corcoran, Janice Battiste

Museyon Guides has made every effort to verify that all information included this
guide is accurate and current as of our press date. All details are subject to change.

PHOTO CREDIT

Page 11 & 110: *THE SEVEN YEAR ITCH*, Marilyn Monroe, Tom Ewell, 1955, © 20th Century Fox Film Corp. /courtesy Everett Collection. Page 12: *MANHATTAN*, Diane Keaton, Woody Allen, 1979, © MGM/ courtesy Everett Collection. Page 14: *KRAMER VS. KRAMER*, Justin Henry, Dustin Hoffman, 1979, © Columbia/courtesy Everett Collection. Page 16: *WHEN HARRY MET SALLY...*, Meg Ryan, Billy Crystal, 1989, © Columbia/courtesy Everett Collection. Page 19: *SEX AND THE CITY: THE MOVIE*, Cynthia Nixon, Kristin Davis, Sarah Jessica Parker, Kim Cattrall, 2008. © New Line Cinema/courtesy Everett Collection. Page 21: *FRIENDS* "Series Finale", Matthew Perry, Lisa Kudrow, David Schwimmer, Courteney Cox Arquette, Jennifer Aniston, Matt LeBlanc, 1994-2004, © Warner Bros. Page 22: *VANILLA SKY*, Tom Cruise, 2001, © Paramount Pictures/courtesy Everett Collection. Page 24: *BIG*, Robert Loggia, Tom Hanks, 1988, © 20th Century Fox Film Corp. / courtesy Everett Collection. Page 27: *BREAKFAST AT TIFFANY'S*, Audrey Hepburn, 1961, courtesy Everett Collection. Page 29: *P.S. I LOVE YOU*, Hilary Swank, Gerard Butler, 2007. © Warner Bros. Page 30: *YOU'VE GOT MAIL*, Tom Hanks, Meg Ryan, 1998. © Warner Bros. Page 32: *INSIDE MAN*, Denzel Washington, director Spike Lee, 2006, photo by Mary Evans/Universal Pictures/Ronald Grant/Everett Collection. Page 34: *I AM LEGEND*, Will Smith, 2007, © Warner Bros. Page 37: *SEINFELD*, Julia Louis-Dreyfus, Larry Thomas as the Soup Nazi, 1990 – 1998, © Columbia TriStar Television/ Courtesy: Everett Collection. Page 39: *NIGHT AT THE MUSEUM*, Ben Stiller, 2006, © 20th Century Fox Film Corp. /courtesy Everett Collection. Page 41: *IT COULD HAPPEN TO YOU*, Nicolas Cage, Bridget Fonda, 1994, © TriStar/courtesy Everett Collection. Page 42: *ANNIE HALL*, Diane Keaton, Woody Allen, 1977, © MGM. Page 44: *TAXI DRIVER*, Robert Deniro, 1976, © Columbia Pictures /courtesy Everett Collection. Page 46: *SINGLE WHITE FEMALE*, Bridget Fonda, 1992. Page 48: *GHOST*, Demi Moore, Patrick Swayze, 1990, © Paramount/courtesy Everett Collection. Page 50: *DEFINITELY, MAYBE*, Ryan Reynolds, Elizabeth Banks, 2008, Photo by: Mary Evans, © 2007 Universal Studios. Page 53: *THE FISHER KING*, Grand Central Station, 1991, courtesy Everett Collection. Page 54: *ONCE UPON A TIME IN AMERICA*, 1984. © Warner Bros./ courtesy Everett Collection. Page 57: *SERENDIPITY*, Kate Beckinsale, John Cusack, 2001, © Miramax. Page 58: *GREAT EXPECTATIONS*, Ethan Hawke, Gwyneth Paltrow, director Alfonso Cuaron, 1998. © 20th Century Fox Film Corp./courtesy Everett Collection. Page 61: *AS GOOD AS IT GETS*, Helen Hunt, Jack Nicholson, Greg Kinnear, 1997, © TriStar Pictures. Page 62: *CROCODILE DUNDEE*, Paul Hogan, 1986, © Paramount Pictures. Page 65: *GHOSTBUSTERS*, Dan Aykroyd, Bill Murray, Harold Ramis, 1984, © Columbia Pictures. Page 67: *SPIDER-MAN*, Tobey Maguire, 2002, © Columbia Pictures/courtesy Everett Collection. Page 69: *SLEEPLESS IN SEATTLE*, Meg Ryan, Ross Malinger, Tom Hanks, 1993, © TriStar Pictures. Page 71: *SCENT OF A WOMAN*, Gabrielle Anwar, Al Pacino, 1992, courtesy Everett Collection. Page 73: *UPTOWN GIRLS*, Brittany Murphy, Dakota Fanning, 2003, © MGM. Page 75: *ONE FINE DAY*, Mae Whitman, George Clooney, Alex D. Linz, Michelle Pfeiffer, 1996, © 20th Century Fox Film Corp./ courtest Everett Collection. Page 77: *HOME ALONE 2*, Macaulay Culkin,

1992, © 20th Century Fox Film Corp. Page 79: *ETERNAL SUNSHINE OF THE SPOTLESS MIND*, Jim Carrey, 2004, © Focus Features/courtesy Everett Collection. Page 81: *MOONSTRUCK*, Cher, 1987, © MGM. Page 83: *THE PROFESSIONAL, (aka LEON)*, Natalie Portman, Jean Reno, 1994, courtesy Everett Collection. Page 85: *AUGUST RUSH*, Jonathan Rhys Meyers, Freddie Highmore, 2007, ©Warner Bros. Page 87: *THE THOMAS CROWN AFFAIR* Pierce Brosnan, 1968, photo by Mary Evans/Ronald Grant/Everett Collection. Page 89: *DESPERATELY SEEKING SUSAN*, Robert Joy, Madonna, 1985, © Orion. Page 91: *SATURDAY NIGHT FEVER*, John Travolta, 1977, courtesy Everett Collection. Page 92: *THE GODFATHER: PART II*, immigrants in Little Italy, NY, in the 1920's, 1974, courtesy Everett Collection. Page 95: *THE GODFATHER PART III*, Andy Garcia, 1990, © Paramount/courtesy Everett Collection. Page 96: *13 GOING ON 30*, Jennifer Garner, Mark Ruffalo, 2004, © Columbia. Page 98: *ACROSS THE UNIVERSE*, Martin Luther, Dana Fuchs, Joe Anderson, T.V. Carpio, Jim Sturgess, 2007. ©Sony Pictures. Page 100: *MIDNIGHT COWBOY*, Jon Voight, Georgann Johnson, 1969, © MGM. Page 102: *THE HOURS*, Meryl Streep, 2002, ©Paramount/courtesy Everett Collection. Page 104: *KATE AND LEOPOLD*, Meg Ryan, Hugh Jackman, 2001, photo by Mary Evans, © Miramax. Page 107: *30 ROCK*, Tracy Morgan, Rachel Dratch, Jack McBrayer, Tina Fey, Alec Baldwin, photo by Mitchell Haaseth, © NBC. Page 109: *THE INTERPRETER*, Sean Penn, 2005, © Universal/courtesy Everett Collection. Page 116: *MAN ON A LEDGE*, from left: Jamie Bell, Elizabeth Banks, 2012, photo by Myles Aronowitz/©Summit Entertainment. Page 120: *24*, *MIDNIGHT COWBOY*, Jon Voight, Dustin Hoffman, 1969, © MGM. *15*, *LETTERS TO JULIET*, Amanda Seyfried, 2010. ©Summit Entertainment. Page 122: *26*, *FAME*, 1980, © Turner Entertainment. *5*, *SEX AND THE CITY 2*, from left: Cynthia Nixon, Sarah Jessica Parker, Kristin Davis, 2010, photo by Craig Blankenhorn/© Warner Bros. Page 125: *8*, *SMASH*, 'Hell on Earth', (Episode 109), Megan Hilty, Katharine McPhee, 2012-, photo by Eric Liebowitz, © NBC. Page 128: *37*, *BREAKFAST AT TIFFANY'S*, Audrey Hepburn, George Peppard, 1961. Page 132: *48*, *GHOSTBUSTERS*, 1984, photo by Mary Evans/Ronald Grant/Everett Collection. Page 135: *57*, *MALCOLM X*, Denzel Washington, 1992, © Warner Bros. *58*, *THE ROYAL TENENBAUMS*, Luke Wilson, Gwyneth Paltrow, Gene Hackman, Ben Stiller, Anjelica Huston, Danny Glover, Kumar Pallana, Grant Rosenmeyer, Jonah Meyerson, 2001 © Touchstone Pictures. Page 144: *71 THE GODFATHER: PART II*, Robert De Niro, 1974, © Paramount Pictures. Page 146: *17 FRIENDS WITH BENEFITS*, Justin Timberlake, Mila Kunis, 2011. Photo by Glen Wilson, ©Screen Gems. Page 147: *THE GODFATHER*, from left: Marlon Brando (on car), John Cazale, on set, 1972, courtesy Everett Collection. *77 THE GODFATHER*, Marlon Brando, John Cazale, 1972, © Paramount Pictures. Page 150: *80 HITCH*, Will Smith, Eva Mendes, 2005, © Columbia Pictures. *82 GHOSTBUSTERS*, Bill Murray, Dan Aykroyd, Harold Ramis, 1984. © Columbia Pictures. Page 154: *83 ANGER MANAGEMENT*, Adam Sandler, Jack Nicholson, 2003, © Columbia Pictures. Other photos by Alex Child, © Museyon.